The Shapiros' Great Menorah Adventure

An Original Illustrated Story Celebrating Hanukkah & Its Traditions

(c) 2020
ISBN 978-1-64252-732-2

Today was the first day of Hanukkah, and Aaron Shapiro couldn't wait!

He hurried downstairs that bright, crisp morning, but he was the first of the kids to wake up.

No one except Benny the dog was in the living room when Aaron got there.

Aaron only had to wait a few minutes, though, for the other Shapiro children to join him.

Soon he heard his little sister Abby and big brother Ethan clomping down the stairs.

Abby and Ethan stretched out on the sofa, but Aaron was too excited to sit down.

That night the first of the menorah candles would be lit, blessings would be said, and the family would eat and have fun together.

Or would they?

Suddenly, the children heard a sharp cry coming from the kitchen!

They rushed in to see their father in a panic.

Beside him on the table was the special storage case where the family's menorah was kept.

But it was empty!

"Oh, dear!" cried the children's father.

"Oh, dear!" cried the children's mother.

Everyone knew the missing menorah was very serious.

Mom and dad had to leave for work and wouldn't be back until nearly sundown, when Hanukkah would begin and the menorah would need to be lit.

What would the Shapiros do?

Abby piped in cheerfully. "Don't worry, mom and dad. Ethan, Aaron and I will search the attic today while you're at work."

"We'll find the menorah for sure!" Abby declared.

The boys were less sure than Abby that they would be able to find the missing menorah, but they went along anyway.

There was nothing else they could do.

They were on holiday from school, so they had all day to search.

Mom said, "Well, Hanukkah is a day of miracles, after all."

Dad said, "We'll just have to have faith that the menorah will turn up in time."

"Don't you worry!" said Abby. "We'll find it!"

Mom and dad left for work, and the children headed to the attic to begin their search.

16-year-old Ethan, the oldest Shapiro child, searched through a big box that was filled with clothes and socks.

There was no menorah.

8-year-old Abby, the youngest Shapiro child, searched through a medium-sized box that was full of books and computer supplies.

There was no menorah.

11-year-old Aaron, the middle Shapiro child, opened a leather case.

Inside there was no menorah, but there was a staff shimmering with light. It was an amazing sight!

Aaron thought suddenly of his namesake, Moses' brother Aaron. That Aaron was famous for having a staff that blossomed miraculously.

Could this staff hold another miracle?

Aaron called his brother and sister over.

As they watched with open mouths, the staff floated up and out of the case in a burst of light.

It was so bright they could hardly see.

Then suddenly, the world became completely dark!

All the children could see was a single oil lantern, floating in front of them.

The lantern had only a tiny flame and was nearly out of oil.

They thought surely it would burn out in a moment and they would be left in utter darkness.

But the light didn't burn out.

Instead, it grew and grew, lighting up the whole, strange world around them. It was so bright all they could see was light.

It reminded the children of the Hanukkah miracle, where the temple light that had only a tiny amount of oil managed to burn for eight days.

Surely this was a sign that they would find the menorah!

When their eyes adjusted to the light, the children saw they were in a wintry kind of place.

There was a path of gelt on the ground beneath their feet. The snow did not stick to the path.

The chocolate coins were huge! They were covered in gold foil and stamped with pictures of menorahs and the Star of David.

Ethan picked up the lantern and said, "Let's go! Surely this is the way to the menorah."

The children had only gone a little way when they found a big pile of gelt.

Next to it were three sacks. One had Ethan's name on it. Another had Aaron's name. The third had Abby's name on it.

Abby couldn't resist picking up a piece of the gelt.

"Someone wants us to have this gelt," she said.

Her brothers didn't argue. Instead, they divided the pile of gelt equally into the three bags.

Although they were tempted to eat some of the gelt, they were in a hurry and didn't want to waste time.

They had promised their parents they would find the family's menorah.

And their mom and dad would not be happy to learn they had been eating chocolate all day!

Aaron led the way back onto the path . . .

. . . and then suddenly they were all falling!

They screamed with surprise, and both of the boys dropped their gelt bags.

Not Abby, though. She loved chocolate too much for that!

Ethan did manage to hold onto the lantern, which he felt sure they needed to light their way and to finish their journey.

Only a few seconds later, the Shapiro kids were dropping down onto a trampoline in a warm, green, fenced yard.

Ethan, Abby, and Aaron were all safe!

They bounced around a little on the trampoline to steady themselves (and because it was it fun).

Their gelt bags and the lantern arrived safely, too. Not a single coin had spilled out from the bags.

The children looked over and saw that someone – or some thing – had appeared to greet them.

It was a dreidel, but a dreidel that had eyes, a mouth, a nose, and a waving hand. It spun around dizzyingly as it welcomed them to this new place.

The dreidel said, "I see that you have the bags of gelt that I left for you. Do you want to play the dreidel game?"

When the children hesitated, the dreidel said, "You have plenty of time, I assure you, and the rest from your travels will do you good."

With the dreidel's reassurance, Abby, Ethan, and Aaron joyfully agreed to a game.

The fall from the sky had been a little unsettling, and a break really would be nice.

Once the children agreed, three other dreidels appeared, each with a Hebrew letter and word on it, so that the children could see all four sides at once.

Nun reminded them that dreidels did not start out as just a fun activity. He explained that a long time ago the Syrians did not allow the Jews to study the Torah. When the soldiers would come by, the Jewish children would hide the Torah and pretend to play with the dreidel.

Nun said that the four Hebrew letters stand for "A Great Miracle Happened There," meaning at the temple with the oil lamp. That is why the dreidel is played during Hanukkah today.

The rules were simple, Shin said. Each child would put one piece of gelt in the center pot. Then they would take turns spinning the dreidel.

If Nun faces up, the player puts nothing in and takes nothing out of the pile.

If Gimmel faces up, the player gets everything in the pot.

If Hay faces up, the player gets half the pot.

If Shin faces up, the player has to put one piece of gelt into the pot.

The children played for a while, but then they began to worry that there wouldn't be enough time for them to find the menorah and get home.

They ended the game with a tie and asked Nun if he could point their way forward on their journey.

Nun said he could do better than that! He snapped his fingers, and a great portal appeared. Nun told them to walk through.

The children waved goodbye and stepped through the door.

Abby, Aaron and Ethan found themselves in a very strange new world.

Nothing looked solid.

A tree stood nearby with sufganiyot - jelly donuts - hanging from its branches.

A sign on a squiggly post said, "eat me."

Abby was suspicious. She reminded her brothers that in the book Alice in Wonderland, cakes that were marked "eat me" made poor Alice grow to be huge.

The boys agreed perhaps it would be better to leave the treats alone.

The Shapiro children moved on a little ways until they came upon a giant, smiling donut with a dollop of jelly on its head for hair.

The donut said, "Welcome to the Land of Sufganiya! Our tasty fried donuts are a reminder of the miraculous oil of Hanukkah! Would you like to try one?" asked the donut.

Abby and Aaron were sorely tempted - they smelled so delicious! - but big brother Ethan told the donut about their quest to find the menorah.

The giant donut smiled and said, "Clearly you must be on your way. I'll be glad to help you!"

The donut gave a whistle, and another donut, this one a unicorn with a hole in its center, appeared.

"Unicorn donuts can fly just like regular unicorns, you know," said the smiling jelly donut.

"Hop aboard and she'll take you straight to Latke Land, which is the next stop on your journey."

Aaron, Abby, and Ethan hopped onto the donut and flew high into the sky.

The unicorn donut set them down on bright orange soil and then flew away. The children gasped at what they saw in this new world.

Before them, a giant, smiling creature that seemed to be made up of shredded potatoes and onions was frying up a big pan of latkes. He was wearing a pink chef's hat, of all things!

"Would you like one of my tasty, fried treats?" the creature asked. "It will fortify you for the rest of your journey."

"Unfortunately, you will have to climb over the pan's bridge and grab one for yourself. I can't do it for you," said the chef. The chef set the pan down on the orange ground.

Ethan was afraid, but he didn't want the younger children to risk hurting themselves. Ethan said he would get a latke for them to share.

Bravely, he climbed onto the bridge and leaped up to take one of the fried potato pancakes.

Surprisingly, the pan wasn't hot at all, even though the oil looked like it was boiling. Ethan easily reached the other end of the bridge and hopped down.

The pink-hatted latke chef congratulated him and pointed toward a path.

"Divide that latke among the three of you and then head that way for a lunch break," said the chef. "Your journey is almost at an end!"

Within in a few moments the children reached a crossroads. There were two signs. One said "applesauce" and the other said "sour cream." "Those are latke toppings!" cried Aaron.

The Shapiro children had never been able to agree what the best latke topping was. This is true in a lot of families.

They agreed to meet back for lunch in five minutes, and then Ethan went off toward the applesauce.

His brother Aaron and sister Abby went off to get some sour cream.

They found a tub with so much sour cream that they went swimming in it!

Abby dunked the latke like it was a basketball.

After a few minutes of playing around, the two kids headed back to where they had agreed to meet Ethan for lunch.

The three children split the latke equally among themselves and sat down on a fallen log to eat.

Ethan dipped his piece in a cup of applesauce he had brought from the applesauce fountain he had visited. It was delicious.

Abby and Aaron ate theirs with dollops of sour cream. Their latkes were also delicious.

After they had eaten, the children got back onto the path, eager to complete their journey and get back home - with the menorah, they hoped.

They had not gone far when they came upon a very strange treehouse in a nearby clearing.

Flour flew from the window like snow.

Golden raisins, and black raisins, and even walnut pieces rained down like hail.

The soft raisins bounced off their heads easily, but those walnuts could hurt!

Just as they were about to run on to save their poor heads, a voice called out from inside the treehouse.

It was a woman's voice, and it seemed familiar.

The voice told them to climb the ladders and come inside.

The children couldn't believe their eyes when they saw their grandmother, Bubbie Asman, inside! It was her voice that they had heard.

Bubbie was making her world-famous rugelach, a family Hanukkah tradition.

The pastry, with its cinnamon, raisins, and nuts, smelled so good that the childrens' stomachs started grumbling even though they had just eaten lunch!

Although the children were glad to see their grandmother, they could not help noticing that the sky outside her kitchen window was starting to dim. Sundown would be here soon.

They told Bubbie Asman about the lost menorah and how worried they were that they wouldn't find it in time.

Bubbie Asman told them not to worry. "Come with me," she said, then led them to the back door of the treehouse and opened it.

A large clock visible through the doorway showed that time was very short.

Swirls of flour suddenly lifted all three children up and through the doorway.

Bubbie Asman waved and said she would see them all again soon! Then she closed the door behind them.

When their eyes adjusted to the dark, Abby, Ethan, and Aaron saw that they were back in their very own attic.

Shadows darkened the room now, but at its center was the family menorah!

Aaron saw that the oil lamp he had carried for so long was gone, but they did not need it to see. Somehow the menorah glowed even though none of its candles were lit.

It was a Hanukkah miracle!

The children carried the menorah downstairs to the living room and put it in the front window for their parents to light after they returned home and sundown arrived.

The Shapiros always put their menorah in the windowsill to spread its light to the world.

Their parents had taught them that Hanukkah is a celebration of miracles, family, faith, and community.

"Chag urim sameach - Happy Festival of Lights," Aaron said with a grin. "Hanukkah sameach - Happy Hanukkah," replied Abby, smiling. "Chag sameac - Happy Holiday," Ethan said with a laugh.

Mom and dad were so happy when they came home and saw the menorah in the window! They were very proud of the children for finding it in time.

At sundown, dad took the shamash candle from the center of the menorah, lit it, and used it to the light the one candle signifying the first of the eight nights of Hanukkah. Tomorrow, they would light two candles, and so on, until they reached the eighth day.

They recited the blessings, played the dreidel game, and ate some of Bubbie's delicious rugelach - perhaps too much!

It was the best Hanukkah ever, Abby thought. They all knew it was a Hanukkah they'd never forget.